The Young Adult's Guide to Financial Independence

Rose C. Wang

Published by Apaira Group LLC, 2024,
2025 Revised Edition.

Table of Contents

ISBN: 979-8-9905494-0-1 [eBook]
ISBN: 979-8-9905494-1-8 [Paperback]
ISBN: 979-8-9905494-2-5 [Hardcover]
ISBN: 979-8-9905494-3-2 [Audiobook]
Printed in the United States of America. Revised edition, June 2025

A special thank you to my family for their encouragement while I undertook this book-writing journey. My children's feedback from a Gen Z perspective was especially helpful in communicating my thoughts. I am especially appreciative of the time you took to support me.

About the Author

ROSE C. WANG IS A SEASONED entrepreneur with over 20 years of experience managing the finances of businesses large and small. Throughout her career, Rose has owned several companies including a thriving manufacturing company and a public accounting firm. This gives her a practical understanding of the financial challenges people face.

Rose has expertise in all aspects of personal finance and entrepreneurship. This includes areas such as budgeting, cash management, and taxes. She is passionate about empowering individuals to achieve their financial goals.

Preface

DURING MY FORMER CAREER as a Certified Public Accountant, I was consistently approached by new graduates and their parents for the best approach to becoming a financially independent adult. These individuals were accomplished in the fields of science, math, engineering, and sales. Yet, managing their finances was frustrating for them.

I started noticing that the questions were the same. This book contains a set of simple tips to help you build the financial foundation to become an independent adult. It is especially helpful for new college graduates trying to make that transition to becoming financially independent adults.

This book is separated into four sections I like to call the Four Pillars of Personal Finance. The first deals with "Managing Money." It covers simple budgeting and banking tips. The second is "Building Wealth Through Retirement Funds." These contain ways to start investing and maximizing the possibility of growth with the power of time. The third is "Establishing Credit for the Future." This section discusses how to lay the foundation for healthy financial credit and how to avoid credit pitfalls. The last bonus section is "Protecting with Insurance." It covers common insurance options and how they can help preserve your assets during unexpected situations.

Managing finances is a learned skill set, especially for someone who is not used to dealing with it. Each tip is simplified into digestible bites that can be implemented at your convenience. Targeting one tip every one or two months can help make the transition smooth. A big thank you to you, my readers, for your willingness to learn. I hope that you can build a foundation that utilizes automation to easily manage and build your finances.

Managing Your Money

Tip 1: Budget with buckets

EVER WONDER "WHERE does all my money go" or "How can I grow my wealth"? When you are in the thick of things dealing with everyday life, managing finances can get cumbersome. Budgeting your monthly income and expenses helps to give you a roadmap to achieving your goal of building wealth.

What is budgeting?

Imagine a nicely baked apple pie. It smells delicious. As you slice each portion, some end up larger than others. You pass them all out to the entire family sitting around the table waiting for their share. In the end, you all enjoy a piece and there is none left. That is, until next month, when you bake the next delicious apple pie.

This is budgeting. The pie is the monthly money you're bringing in. The family is every part of your financial life that is important to you. The total pie size is set, but you can always adjust the individual piece size. Your job is to ensure everyone gets a piece of the pie before it's gone.

The same theory holds true for monthly budgeting. When your monthly income is steady, figuring out how to allocate what you have to all the important areas of your life is when wealth-building really begins.

The bucket trick

The key to budgeting is making it easy and automated. Here is a simple trick to help you manage your money and keep you on track with your budget. I refer to it as budgeting with buckets. When I say buckets, I *really* mean different money accounts. The goal is to have four accounts designated for a specific purpose. Funding them is in the following respective order:

1. **One checking account for needs.**
2. **One savings account for wants.**
3. **One high yield saving account for emergency funds.**
4. **One brokerage account for wealth building.**

Once these are opened, set up your paycheck direct deposit to fund each account according to what you budget for.

The spending accounts

The needs account is prioritized first. Add up what you estimate spending monthly on rent, mortgage, utilities, insurance, car payments, groceries, general clothing, healthcare, debt, transportation, insurance, etc. These are normally recurring charges for the basics so that you will have a roof over your head, food on the table, and clothes on your back.

Write them out or put them on a Google Sheet. List all the recurring charges that happen monthly. Include the expenses that do not happen monthly (i.e. car insurance or property taxes). Sometimes it helps to review your bank transactions to see what expenses there were over the last 6 months. Once you have this list, you now have an idea of how much to fund your needs bucket monthly. This needs account will fill and drain every month. Because this account is not meant to grow and so many transactions flow in and out, it is best as a checking account.

Secondly, is the wants account. Funding a wants bucket next is contrary to popular belief. I believe that since I work hard for my money, I should have some enjoyment to keep me going. Develop a 6-month target of what you want to do with your wants fund. Taking a weekend trip? Eyeing that designer outfit? You work hard for your money, you are living your young adult life, and you should enjoy it to help you stay motivated to work. 5% of your net paycheck is a good percentage to start with. This wants account should be filled every month and drained at the end of 6 months (when you treat yourself!). Because this account is short term, it is best as a savings account. This way you can earn some interest before the 6-month target.

The safety net

Next, put any excess money into building an emergency fund. A good rule of thumb is to save at least 6 months' salary in the emergency fund. Once the emergency fund is fully funded, you can reallocate the excess funds to the wealth fund. The purpose of this fund is to cover the unexpected situations that arise in life. For example, should you ever find yourself downsized, needing to stop employment for several months, facing a major repair, or dealing with unexpected medical expenses, this emergency fund will give you peace of mind that you can take some time to deal with the situation. I recommend holding this fund in a high yield savings that is FDIC insured. This will allow the flexibility to access the funds immediately while keeping them secure and earning a higher interest rate since they will be held in perpetuity.

The wealth builder

If you are lucky enough to have excess left over, allocate it into your wealth fund. 10%-15% of a net paycheck is a lofty but attainable goal. The higher the percentage, the closer you are to independent wealth. I recommend investing this money in a brokerage account. If you are just starting out, save yourself the higher fees and start with a reputable, self-serve brokerage house such as Charles Schwab, Vanguard, Fidelity, TD Ameritrade, etc. These are just options, and I am not recommending them exclusively over other brokerage houses. They have zero-to-low cost mutual funds, Exchange Traded

Funds (ETFs), bonds, and Certificate of Deposits from various investments all under one company. This makes it easier to grow with them. As you accumulate more, you can transition to professional management of your account.

Here is the important part about this wealth bucket. As your income grows, the level of your needs bucket may not grow as dramatically. **Thus, this wealth bucket is positioned to catch all the excess funds**. Maybe that 10%-15% you used to allocate to wealth is now 20%-25%. Thus, the wealth bucket should be positioned to grow the most.

Summary

Using four separate money accounts creates an automated system that manages how you decided to spend and save your money. Because the four accounts are physically separated, there is not an easy way to mix them. It builds walls between what was budgeted for that financial life slice. Can you transfer between funds if you need to? Sure. It just makes the action intentional, so you are aware when your spending is different from your budget.

Tip 2: Automate
your money

ONCE ALL YOUR RESPECTIVE bucket accounts are established, automating all your deposits and the major expenses put your budgeting on autopilot. I recommend that you try to automate all payroll deposits and regular bill payments. This will simplify managing your finances for the year. Tips for automation are:

Activate paycheck direct deposit with your employer. Set up your paycheck direct deposits to allocate the dollar amount you want to go into your respective buckets: needs (single or joint, if applicable), wants, emergency fund, and wealth building. Normally, you can choose one bank account for any excess funds. For this situation, select your emergency funds account until it hits the level equivalent to 6 months' salary. Thereafter, you can change it to fund your wealth-building account.

Some employers have a limit on the number of direct deposit accounts allowed or do not offer direct deposit. In these cases, you can always deposit into one checking account. Then create repetitive auto transfers into the other bucket accounts for the next day.

Activate online banking bill payment or automatic draw for all recurring payments on the needs account. Some banks will charge a fee for online bill payment, some will not. Double check with your bank and see whether it makes sense if the costs are worth the convenience for you. Normally, most vendors will allow for a draw from your bank account without any fees or for a minimal charge. For example, I normally see vendors collecting rent, electricity, cell phone bills, insurance, and debt payments with auto draw from your needs account and on a specific date without charge. Check with each respective vendor you are working with and go from there. Many vendors have bill pay incorporated within their online sites.

Keep a starting cushion balance of $500.00 on all needs accounts. Dates of when paychecks are deposited and when bills are paid may differ. It is a good idea to start the fund with an extra cushion of at least $500.00 to catch any of these timing differences. This cushion can reduce the risk of going cash negative. If you start to notice that your needs account dips below your $500 cushion often, it may be time to re-evaluate your budget. Are there new needs that were not accounted for? Are your wants mixing into the needs category? It is your money, so adjust your automatic direct deposits and payment as you care for your current and future lifestyle. I recommend at least evaluating your budget and adjustments annually.

Pro tip: Some banks also require a minimum daily balance. If this is your bank, ensure to add the $500.00 cushion on top of your minimum required balance.

Summary

If you have all your funds automatically going into your buckets, it acts as a simple form of budgeting. Automating the payments and deposits puts most of your budget on autopilot. This system helps build the foundation of your needs, wants, and wealth building goals.

Tip 3: Find harmony
in cohabitation

FINANCES CAN CAUSE strain on all relationships. This is because budgeting jointly is different than budgeting for an individual. One person's wants may be another person's needs and vice versa. Cohabitation with your significant other, spouse, or roommate is so much easier when the financial rules are agreed upon and determined upfront.

Communication and automation of bill payments can give the couple more time to focus on more important matters like the relationship. The goal is to find financial harmony during cohabitation. This tip relates only to addressing the "needs" bucket.

Sit down and have the "talk." This step is the most critical of all. Because it is normally treated as a social taboo to discuss money with those you love. It is important to have that talk early and figure out a plan to implement your agreement easily. Write down exactly what will be paid out of the joint needs bucket (i.e., housing, rent, utilities, etc.). I want to stress that these are basic joint needs that all involved will share. There will be some gray areas that inherently are uneven (like groceries, dining out, gas, etc.). Someone may eat more or have a more expensive taste than another. One party may need to drive further to work than another. All these situations should be addressed in this talk and written down. Items that are deemed necessary by only one partner only would fall into the "wants' category for that individual. Once you figure out your joint needs bucket, outline how much each party can allocate to cover the bucket monthly.

Once the contribution and payment items are settled, I congratulate you. Have all parties sign and date your agreement. I know this seems uneasy and weird, but it will help to have it in writing should you need to refer to it later. It will help to keep harmony in the future. As I mentioned, the needs bucket is the main one to be concerned about for financial harmony.

Instead of an individual needs account, create a joint needs checking account bucket. All shared expenses should be paid from the joint account only. If you anticipate being short on some months (like unexpected house repair), all parties involved will still put the extra funds in this joint checking account, as agreed upon. The reason for keeping everything flowing through this account is "accountability" and "record-keeping."

Everyone has access to the account so everyone can see what is going in and out of it. To this point, everyone on the account can also draw from it. Only open a joint account with someone that you trust, and you project to be in your life in the long term. To limit risk, I would not activate an overdraft on this account.

Keep your individual want buckets. As I mentioned, this tip concentrates primarily on the cohabitation "needs" category only. The reason is all parties need to find common ground. The basic cohabitation 'needs" is far easier to agree on than the cohabitation "wants." Being able to manage how you spend your disposable money without scrutiny is your right. Everyone's choices and opinions on how to spend disposable income are different. Retaining separation of individual want buckets is a way to further promote harmony in a joint relationship.

If you want to make a joint wants and wealth bucket, feel free to put it down in writing. You can apply these steps as well, but it is not as critical for financial harmony.

Summary

The goal of managing the needs funds jointly is having financial harmony in the house. Hopefully, this will help to free your minds of managing the basic needs long enough to focus on the more important matters of the relationship.

Tip 4: Review bank transactions monthly

NOW THAT YOU HAVE ALL your accounts automatically set up to fund and pay from your respective buckets, you are ready to take this one step further by reviewing your income and expenses monthly. Performing your review will help you to find errors timely and give insight as to where your money comes from and goes.

How to reconcile bank accounts

Reconciling your bank account has never been easier with online banking tools. Most online banking websites allow you to login and access your bank transactions in real time. Many show a daily trail of deposits and withdraws, pending transactions, and allow you to even conduct filtered searches.

With your buckets set up, the easiest way to review your charges and deposits in each account is online or in your banking app. It is best to review your account at least monthly. Scan through the daily transaction log for that month. If most of the transactions are recurring or automated, it should be easier to spot any transactions that you do not recognize.

What to do when something is unrecognized

If you notice an unrecognized transaction, research it, and report it to your bank as soon as possible. If the unrecognized charge is done via electronic funds transfer, the bank generally allows you 60 days from the date of the bank statement to dispute the unrecognized transaction.[1] Various other laws apply depending on how the charge was processed by the bank. Therefore, it is recommended to notify the bank as soon as an error is noticed.

This method of review is a simplistic way to reconcile your bank accounts. It is good to use when managing a lower number of bank accounts.

When to consider financial software

Once the number of accounts you manage increases to over ten, you may want to consider utilizing financial software to help manage and reconcile them. Financial software allows you to visually combine all your different bank accounts in a dashboard, view daily transactions, and track your spending by categories. Tracking your funds is easily done with online financial software, online checkbooks, and the like. When you pair this software with digital downloads of your banking and credit card transactions, you can easily allocate categories for all your monthly expenses. This also makes reconciling your bank account simpler. Many banks even offer automatic reconciliations with your financial software.

These software programs are sometimes free to low cost for the basic versions. Examples of financial software are Quicken or Mint (now integrated into Credit Karma) by Intuit. These are just options, and I am not recommending them exclusively over other financial software. The main drawback of some of the free versions is it may not allow you to enter checks or charges that have not yet run through the bank. Thus, you may not have an accurate cash balance.

Should you want to track your uncleared checks, uncleared charges, or create budgeting reports, you may want to look at paid software. One example is Quicken. Quicken allows you to enter all charges and reconcile them with the cleared bank transaction. It also has bill pay capabilities, budgeting upcoming expenses, income and expense reports, stock, and investment tracking. It can be tracked on your desktop or synced to the web. As a bonus, it can sync with their tax product. All these features come at a cost. When you have multiple wealth accounts in your portfolio, I believe it is also worth considering utilizing a type of financial software to track their worth.

Summary

Reconciling your bank accounts monthly helps to identify errors sooner. The advent of online banking apps makes reviewing charges and deposits more efficient. It is one more tool in managing your funds for accuracy. It also helps you to understand the timing of when your funds flow in and out. Understanding this timing also promotes cash management.

Tip 5: Save on bank fees

BANKS MAKE SOME OF their money by charging customers monthly banking fees. The most common banking fees are listed here: monthly banking, overdraft, and out-of-network ATM cash withdrawal fees. More fees can be charged, but these are the most common. Let's discuss what these fees are and how to avoid them.

Monthly maintenance fees

Monthly maintenance fees are the bank's charges for holding your funds. Typically, this is assessed on checking accounts and low-balance savings accounts. Maintaining at least three bank accounts, each with monthly bank fees could potentially add up. I have recently seen these fees range from $7 to as high as $29 each month.

One of the best ways to avoid these fees is to **choose a bank that will waive these maintenance fees** if you meet their minimum transaction or balance levels. Some examples I have seen include having monthly automatic paycheck deposits over a certain dollar threshold or keeping a minimum daily dollar amount in the account or all combined with the bank. With tip 2 automation of your money, you could easily qualify for the automatic paycheck deposit option. If you are in college, I have seen some banks offer students no minimum balance bank accounts with no maintenance fees. Look for a reputable bank that you can grow with that will offer a waiver of the monthly maintenance fees.

Overdraft fees

Overdraft fees normally occur when a bank account has tried to go cash negative. Some examples of this are if there are not enough funds in your bank account to cover a check presented, another bank draw (like a monthly maintenance fee), or a deposit you previously made is reversed thus making your bank balance negative. If you write a check and your checking account does not have enough money in the account to cover it, the bank will not pay out the funds and return the check to the presenter (a.k.a. bounced check). Because their bank had to spend their time fixing the issue, they normally charge an "overdraft fee." I have seen some overdraft fees as high as $35.00 each day the account is overdrawn. The fee is quite high and meant to act as a deterrent.

How can you avoid these overdraft fees? There are a couple of ways. First, you can only use a debit card for all your purchases. A debit card allows you to physically access your funds electronically at the store register with your PIN. If the purchase you are making exceeds the amount of funds you have in the bank, the store will automatically reject that transaction. The good news is you can never go beyond your available cash balance. The bad news is the embarrassment of having your payment rejected at a restaurant and having to borrow money from your date or friends to pay it. The better alternative is to **sign up for "overdraft" protection** on your checking account.

When you sign up (or opt-in) for overdraft protection on your checking account, the bank is extending you a small line of credit to help avoid an accidental or occasional overdraft. If your balance goes negative, the bank will pay out the check or debit card transaction and draw on that small overdraft line of credit. Be aware that the line of credit is small, and the loan interest percentage is high. The best way to use this overdraft protection is as an insurance policy. It is good to have but not to use. Make it a habit to reconcile your bank account and immediately pay off the overdraft line once it kicks in.

Out-of-network ATM cash withdrawal fee

I have noticed that with the advent of person-to-person payment apps (like Venmo, PayPal, Zelle, etc.) and the wide adoption of credit card payments, there is less of a need to withdraw physical cash from the bank. When you do need to withdraw cash from the ATM (Automatic Teller Machine), you can normally take money out of your account at your bank, all their branches, and in network banks without paying an ATM cash withdrawal fee. Currently, I have seen total fees range from $2.00 - $7.00 per transaction. Let's say you are at an international concert and need to withdraw some cash. If the nearest ATM is "out-of-network" with your bank, then you may end up paying these different types of fees:

- Processing ATM fee: a fee for the bank that owns

that ATM. Normally, the machine will alert you of their ATM processing fee at the time of withdrawal.

- Out-of-network fee: your bank charges a processing fee for the out-of-network withdrawal.
- International ATM fee: Since you are traveling out of the country, there may also be an additional international transaction fee charged by your bank.

With a little bit of planning, here are three ways to avoid or limit paying these ATM cash withdrawal fees.

1. **Only utilize ATMs that are in-network:** Your banking app or website can tell you where the closest in-network ATM is. Going to your bank and its branches is a good place to start.

2. **Get cash back at a store:** If you are paying with your debit card at a large chain store, they may give you the option to withdraw cashback during checkout. The withdrawal is normally limited to low dollar amounts of around $20.00 to $60.00. For example, if you purchase groceries for $27.00 and choose a cashback of $20.00, the store will charge your debit card $47.00 and give you $20.00 in cash. If you choose this option, I suggest doing the checkout at the in-person cashier to confirm you get your cash back.

3. **Work with a bank that reimburses ATM out-of-network fees:** Some banks offer reimbursement of the out-of-network fee as a part of their banking package. The processing and international fees may or

may not be reimbursed depending on the banking package. Because this is after-the-fact reimbursement, this option may just limit your fees, not avoid it altogether.

Summary

Bank fees every month can add up. This is especially true if you have multiple bank accounts (buckets). Choosing bank programs that allow a waiver of monthly maintenance fees is a great option to reducing your expenses. Opting in for overdraft protection and planning cash withdrawals also help to save on bank fees. A little bit saved every month can add up over the years. Reinvesting those saved expenses is a great start to building your wealth.

Tip 6: Designate a beneficiary

LIFE IS UNPREDICTABLE and things happen. Planning for the unforeseeable future can save your loved one's future heartache. As you start to open your bank and investment accounts, there is one simple step that can be taken to ease the transfer of those assets should something happen to you. It is known as adding a beneficiary designation to all your accounts.

A beneficiary is defined as someone who will take ownership of that asset after the passing of the original owner. Most times a beneficiary will be a real person. Some banks may allow a company or trust. Note: If your estate planning is further along and you have a revocable trust set up, this chapter may not be as pertinent to you. Also, estate planning is extraordinarily complex, so this simple tip applies only to financial institutions on personal accounts. Always seek a professional for your specific situation.

Why do it?

If a personal financial account does not have a beneficiary designation, the assets would fall under the probate laws. These laws are formed to assist in the transfer of a deceased's property.

Most US states will have varying probate laws. Depending on the state and complexity of the assets involved, probate can normally take an average of 6 to 24 months. During this time, the financial assets are controlled by the financial institution. This makes it difficult for the beneficiaries or family of the deceased to access funds needed for basics like rent, funeral costs, credit card payments, etc. If the account has a beneficiary designation, the transfer is outside of the probate laws. It is normally much quicker and taken care of right at the financial institution.

How to do it?

The terminology used when working with the bank is adding a beneficiary, ITF (In Trust For), or POD (Payable On Death) designation on the account. Before setting up your beneficiaries, gather the following key information:

- Full name (including middle names). This should be the same as their legal identification (i.e., passport, driver's license, state identification, or birth certificate)
- Current address
- Phone number
- Legal identification for the beneficiaries. This requirement depends on the financial institution's policy. I have had some request it and others not.

Pro tip: Most financial institutions will allow adding a beneficiary, but some may limit the type of accounts you can add it to. I have seen some institutions limit beneficiaries on checking accounts, while others will allow it on all accounts.

When do I do it?

Ideally, it is best to add your beneficiaries when you first open your accounts. It does not matter how small your fund balance is in the beginning. You are in the process of growing your wealth. This balance may be significantly larger later in your life. If you already have accounts established, then discuss the process of adding the beneficiaries with your financial institutions. After you set them up, know that you should be able to change your beneficiaries at any time.

Summary

No one ever really wants to talk about what will happen after they are gone. Maybe we have this innate feeling that we may live forever. This step is not for your benefit. It is for the benefit of those that must pick up the pieces, settle your holdings, all while they mourn. I have seen families torn up by the responsibility and decision making that they are not ready for. This is an easy tip to use for you and your loved one's future peace of mind.

Tip 7: Build a strong banking relationship

BUILDING A RELATIONSHIP with your local branch can set you up for success later in life – especially when you are ready to apply for a mortgage, open a line of credit, or expand into business banking. Your goal is to find a banking partner that is right for you and helps save, or even make, you money. On the flip side, the banker is also looking to establish long-term relationships that increase their assets under management. They want your savings, credit card, mortgage, and brokerage business because those assets help to generate income for the bank. When it works, it is a mutually beneficial relationship.

Why it is important

When you set out to build your bank relationship, I found it advantageous to have a physical branch you can go into with a strong online platform. If something goes wrong, it is incredibly helpful to have a banker that personally knows you and your financial patterns. I am aware of many situations where bankers were an additional line of defense in potentially fraudulent financial withdrawals.

Looking ahead, that relationship can help later in life when you are ready for major financial steps, like buying a car, securing a mortgage, or opening a business line of credit. Like any relationship, trust takes time to build. The earlier you start, the better positioned you will be when you need support. Selecting a banker is like any relationship. They should relate well with you, understand your goals, and know their banking product enough to alert you to special promotions or opportunities.

Getting started

Do you like coupons or those loyalty points you earn from airlines? I know I do. Why should banking be any different? Some banks have been known to offer attractive sign-up bonuses or loyalty rewards to bring in new customers. Look around for deals that reward you now, keep your bank monthly fees at a minimum, and help you set a good foundation for a strong banking relationship. Some examples of bank promotions are:

- cash bonuses for the opening of new accounts
- waiver of monthly fees with minimum balance and direct deposits
- reward points for funds on account and debit card transactions.
- An easy online search can bring several opportunities. Go with a bank that is large enough in your regional area to accommodate ATMs for cash withdrawals, limit your monthly maintenance fees, and allow for interbank electronic transfers. If you can find a

program with no monthly fees, that is the best option. The more you bank with them, the more you may be rewarded.

Summary

Laying the foundations for a solid banking relationship early on can play a key role in supporting your financial journey. Look for a banker who understands your goals and a bank that values your loyalty. This mutually beneficial relationship can be invaluable when you're ready to make significant financial decisions, such as leasing a car, buying a home, or starting a business.

Building Wealth Through Retirement Fund

Tip 8: Invest Early in a Roth IRA or Roth 401(k)

A RETIREMENT FUND IS money earned from wages that an individual sets aside to help sustain their livelihood after age 59.5. Because the US government wants you to be able to stand on your own feet when you are no longer of working age, they built tax incentives to encourage its citizens to save. IRA (Individual Retirement Account) and 401K are two types of the most common retirement accounts allowed in the United States. The general principles for an IRA and 401K are similar plans. A 401K is managed by your employer. IRAs are managed by the individual. All retirement funds fall under two tax categories: tax deferred and after tax. Let's start with learning the basic definition of these categories:

Tax-deferred: Tax-deferred (pre-tax) account examples include traditional Individual Retirement Accounts (IRA), 401(k), SEP, SIMPLE, and 403(b) accounts. Funds contributed to the account are excluded from taxable wages for the designated year it is contributed to. Taxes are paid on the contribution and any subsequent growth earned when the funds are withdrawn from the account.

After-tax: After-tax accounts include ROTH IRA and ROTH 401(k) accounts. Taxes are paid upfront, but only on the initial contributions to the account. The great benefit of this account is that the account can grow tax-free for all subsequent years. No further taxes are paid when qualified funds are withdrawn no matter how large the fund grows. Note: current guidelines restrict qualified withdrawals until after age 59.5 and a five-year holding period. There are some exceptions that apply[2].

Choosing between tax-deferred or after-tax

Selecting the type of retirement contribution to make comes down to your specific taxable income situation for the year. Once you are no longer a "dependent" for tax purposes, here are two general tips on when to use each option:

1. **Tax-deferred for those individuals at or higher than the median tax rate:** Since this option reduces the taxable wages in the year it is contributed to, it is a good option for high-earning individuals at or higher than the median tax rate bracket. As your income grows, you may move into higher tax brackets. Then, tax deference options like traditional IRAs or 401Ks may help to move you back into lower tax brackets.

2. **After-tax for younger individuals earning less than the median tax rate:** This option is most beneficial earlier in your life when you have a lower income and more time for the asset to grow. It is normally a good

option for part-time workers. It is also a good option for college students during their first partial year of high-wage full-time employment (i.e., for those that graduate in May and start full-time employment halfway into the calendar year). If you do not need the extra funds now and can afford to pay the tax on this income, this is a good option for those below the median tax rate bracket.

Benefits of after-tax contributions

The primary benefit of an after-tax Roth IRA or Roth 401K is that any accumulated growth in those funds will not be taxed when you withdraw them within the withdrawal rules. This allows you to keep that built-up wealth for the future.

Another significant benefit happens when you begin receiving USA social security benefits in retirement. Whether those benefits are taxable depends on your total income and benefits for that year. Go over a designated income threshold and some of those benefits may become taxable.[3] However, qualified withdrawals from a Roth account are not currently included as income for that calculation. Note this is the current US tax situation, but tax laws are constantly changing. Be sure to consult with your tax advisor as it applies to your situation. Keeping your social security non-taxable can potentially save more money in your pocket later in life.

Summary

IRAs are retirement accounts set up by individuals. 401Ks are set up by employers. Both may offer tax deferred or after-tax (Roth) contributions. If you do not need the extra funds, it is smart to start contributing to a Roth retirement plan in the lower-earning years. Then, when your earnings reach the median tax rate bracket or higher, consider switching to a traditional retirement plan. While Roth contributions are taxed up front, the benefit is that they grow tax-free. If your earnings are low enough, the tax rate should also be lower. Starting early with a Roth allows your investments to grow tax-free for a longer period. The current upside is enjoying tax-free withdrawals of those earnings in retirement.

Tip 9: Free money
for retirement

FUNDING YOUR RETIREMENT accounts is normally done with your earnings. What would you think if I told you there was a way to have 'free' money for your retirement contribution? Here is one option to help you earn additional funds to contribute to your retirement account.

Through a Company match

Today, many employers offer a company matching program on any employee retirement contribution. If you contribute a part of your paycheck to your retirement fund, the company will match that contribution up to a designated percentage or amount. Why would a company do this? There are many reasons, one being to retain employees. Another reason is due to the governing Employee Retirement Income Security Act (ERISA) top-heavy rules ensuring that lower-paid employees receive a minimum benefit if there are larger contributions to key employees. Regardless of why, it is to your benefit to always contribute to your retirement fund up to the company match amount. That is a 100% growth of your money instantly.

One thing to be aware of is the company's minimum vesting period. The company may match your retirement contribution annually, but you will not earn their contribution until you have been employed by that company for at least their designated number of years. The terminology to describe this situation is called "vesting." If you leave prematurely or do not qualify for the Company's other minimum requirements, you will not receive the Company matching funds. Those non-vested funds will be returned to the Company. Please note that you will still retain the amount of money that you personally contributed to the retirement fund.

Summary

Looking for these opportunities to get ahead with your retirement can help form a solid foundation for your wealth bucket. If your employer offers a retirement account with matching contributions, it is a great wealth building opportunity to contribute enough to get the full match. Who wouldn't want an instant return on their money?

Tip 10: Simplify
your investments

ONCE YOU HAVE MADE your contribution to your retirement account, you have the fun part of investing it. Every investment carries some level of risk and corresponding reward. The higher the risk, normally the higher the reward. Here is a very brief overview of the 5 general types of investing classes and how they typically generate income:

- Cash
- Bonds
- Stocks
- Physical assets
- Intangible assets

Cash

We all are used to spending cash on everyday goods and services. It is a country's tangible currency. This includes currency in your wallet, bank, savings, CD, and brokerage cash accounts. Cash held in Federal Deposit Insurance Corporation (FDIC) -insured bank accounts are insured from bank failure by the US government up to a specified limit. The current basic amount of protection is currently $250,000 per owner for all combined accounts held in that FDIC-insured banking institution. This amount of protection can vary based on the number of account owners, beneficiaries, and number of accounts at the institution. The FDIC government website has a convenient calculator to assist with your specific limit[4]. This protection does not cost the owner anything.

Pro tip: Because Fintech company apps (like Venmo) are not banks, the cash held in these companies may not be FDIC-insured. The better protection practice is to transfer your funds in these apps to a linked FDIC-insured bank systematically and often.

The primary way to make money from this investment is through interest earned. When you deposit your cash into a savings account or CD, the bank will pay you interest on your cash balance. Payment is usually calculated daily and paid out monthly into that same account.

Bonds

Bonds are loans from an investor to a borrower (issuer) for a set amount of time at a stated return of interest rate (coupon). After the contracted borrowing time has passed (matures), the issuer promises to return the principal (par or face value) to the investor on record. Examples of bond issuers are government divisions (Federal, State, County, municipality, or agency) or corporations. These issuers sell these bonds to the public to raise money for general or capital funds.

The most common way to make money on a bond purchase is to earn interest until it matures. How often interest is paid is also stated in the bond contract. This payment term can range from monthly, quarterly, semiannually, annually, or upon maturity. Let's look at an example of a bond purchase and redemption:

Issuer: US Treasury

Par (face value): $25,000.00

Date of issue: 3/12/24

Maturity: 3/12/26

Coupon: 4.2%

Payment term: Semi-annual

In this example above, let's assume the purchaser bought this bond on the date of issue directly from the US Treasury. The purchaser would loan $25,000.00 to the US Treasury by purchasing this bond. They would expect to receive $2100.00 of interest paid out bi-annually at $525.00. On 3/12/26, the purchaser would anticipate receiving back the par value of $25,000.00. This is the end of the loan period and transaction.

What about a bond that has a "zero" coupon interest rate? This terminology is commonly used for short-term US Treasury Bills. It means no interest is earned on the bond. The purchaser makes money by buying the bond at a percentage lower than 100% of the face value (i.e. 95.8%). This is known as a discount. When the bond matures, the purchaser is paid 100% of the face value.

Stocks

Stocks can be shares of publicly traded companies. When a company is publicly traded, they are offering the purchaser the ability to buy shared ownership of that company. You are known as their shareholder even if you own one share of this company. Being a shareholder entitles you to vote in the annual shareholder meeting and receive any shareholder dividends. You also risk losing your investment if that company goes bankrupt or delisted. Note that you can also buy stocks in privately owned companies (such as hedge funds or private businesses), but we will not discuss them in this book as they are not easily obtainable nor open to investment by most of the public. The simplest method to buy and hold these publicly traded shares is in your brokerage account.

Pro tip: When selecting a brokerage firm to use, look for established brokerages with enough Securities Investor Protection Corporation (SIPC) Insurance to cover the value of your brokerage accounts. This insurance was created by a consortium of private brokerage companies to self-insure their members from brokerage failure or default. It is privately insured and not a government-backed insurance form of protection.

One common way to make money on stocks is through dividends. If a company is profitable, it can choose to share that profit with their shareholders through dividends. The amount is determined by the company's Board of Directors. A dividend is calculated at an amount per share multiplied by the number of shares. It can be an amount or percentage per shared owned.

Whichever shareholder holds the share of stock by the cutoff (ex-dividend) date earns the dividend. They are normally paid quarterly and deposited into your brokerage account that holds the related stock share.

Another way to make money on stocks is through the price difference from what you bought it at and what you sold it at. The value of publicly traded stocks fluctuates constantly. Unless you are purchasing the stock directly from the company itself, you are likely to buy it through a stock exchange. The value is determined by the mutual transaction price the last seller and buyer agreed upon. If you can sell your stock at a higher price than you initially purchased it for, you make money (profit).

Physical assets

Physical assets are tangible items you can see and touch assets. Examples include real estate, precious metals, rare coins, collectible sports cards, vintage toys, and artwork. To protect it, store it safely and maintain it well. If it is valuable, consider insuring it in case of accident, theft, or destruction.

One way to make money on physical assets is through the price difference from what you bought it at and what you sold it at. Another way is to rent or lease out the asset to another. Common physical assets that are rented are real estate or automobiles.

Intangible assets

Intangible assets are intellectual property. Most intangible assets are developed by individuals or companies. It is hard to describe because they cannot be physically held in your hand. Examples of intangible assets are copyrighted music, literary work, goodwill, and software.

One way to make money on intangible assets is through the sale of the rights to use that asset to another person or entity. This is known as royalty income. Although this class of assets is too specialized to discuss at this level, I still wanted you to be aware that this is also a class of assets.

Simplify investing in stocks and bonds

Let me reiterate that every investment comes with the opportunity for risk or reward. For stocks and bonds, there are many options to invest your funds from very conservative to extremely aggressive. Deciding how to invest in these depends on your risk tolerance for losing and expectations for gains.

To simplify your investments, you may consider starting with Exchange-Traded Funds (ETF) or mutual funds. These are pooled funds managed by investment companies that purchase a basket of stocks, bonds, or both.

The advantages of both ETFs and mutual funds are they allow you to start with lower amounts of initial funds and for consistent, automated investment. The disadvantage of mutual funds is that the price for purchases is determined only at the end of each investing day. Essentially, you buy and sell during the day without knowing the actual final price. Conversely, ETFs allow you to designate your purchase and sale price that you are willing to pay. Because of this control, ETFs normally are more beneficial in the long term.

As you research how to invest your wealth funds, here are some simple tips to keep in mind:

1. **Consider Index funds for broad-based, simplified investing.** Everyday news will normally mention the daily fluctuation of common broad-based indexes. Examples are the Standard and Poor's 500 (S&P 500), Dow Jones Industrial Average (DJIA), and NASDAQ Composite. Many EFTs and mutual funds mimic these common indexes. Investing in funds that track broad based indexes will give you a general idea of how your investments are doing daily.

2. **Consider Target Date funds (TDF) for automated risk adjustment.** If you have an idea of the year you would like to retire, TDF are an interesting option. They normally hold a blend of stocks, bonds, and other investments. As time reaches the target date, the fund will adjust the blend held to try and select less risky holdings. TDF are normally useful for longer term investment time frames like retirement or college fund target dates.

3. **Consider balancing with bonds.** Traditionally, bonds are less risky than stocks. AAA and AA grade bonds are examples of traditionally lower-risk bond options. There are EFTs and mutual funds that mimic these bond options. The goal is to use these to

keep up with inflation and try to balance your overall risk.

4. **Identify low expense ratio funds.** The annual cost an investor will pay for fund management is presented as a percentage called the "expense ratio." This cost adds up over the years. It can impact the fund's dividend income paid out to you and asset value. To keep the cost of your investment lower, consider those funds with low expense ratios and a good 5- or 10-year return record.

5. **Understand the fund's sales fee.** The sales fee of a fund is calculated as a percentage of your investment called a "load." It is charged to you when you buy (front-end), sell (back-end), or neither (no-load) a fund. A no-load fund typically incorporates their sales fee within their expense ratio or other daily management expenses fees. Identifying the fund load helps you with cash flow by knowing when you will be paying these sales fees.

What about individual stocks and physical assets?

As you get more comfortable with investing, you may think about investing in other traditional areas like individual stocks or physical assets. Here are some general tips while you advance to investing in these:

For individual stocks, consider waiting until you gain medium investing experience (5 years into investing). This gives you time to get a feeling about how world economics, politics, and other macroeconomics like inflation influence stocks and bonds returns. Limit this to 10-15% of your total investments to help reduce risk. Research what you know and companies you use.

For physical assets, calculate the annual cost of maintaining that asset before purchasing it. Examples of usual costs include insurance, common area maintenance fee, operating cost like gas or electricity, and interest expense. Include this cost in your decision prior to purchasing the investment asset.

Summary

Every investment comes with the opportunity for risk or reward. Before investing, consider the investment's objectives, risks, charges and expenses. Read any investment prospectus or summaries. It is absolutely OK to ask your questions to the investment company before you decide. It is your money, and you should feel comfortable with your decisions.

Start with the level at which you are comfortable accepting the related risk of loss. As your wealth becomes more established, consider working with a reputable financial planner to develop your wealth building plan.

Tip 11: Automate investing strategies

IN INVESTING, TIME is your friend. The longer your money stays invested, the higher the chance it can grow. Here are two simple strategies to enact when you start investing in your wealth bucket.

Dollar-cost averaging is the consistent investment of the same amount at the same interval of time. One example is purchasing $100 every month in the same group of mutual funds/ETFs consistently. The theory here is that by investing on a schedule one can catch the ups and downs of the market. You may purchase some shares when it is depressed or when it is high. The hope is your purchases balance out over the years and keep you investing for long term growth. Being consistent with the dollar amount and time between purchases are the key factors in this investment strategy.

Your strategy on purchases can be every paycheck, monthly, quarterly, or annually. It is entirely up to you. Remember if time is on your side, investing through downturns will help you to purchase more shares in hopes of future appreciation. This "set it and forget it" method of investing is an easy approach for anyone to follow.

Dividend reinvestment is a way to increase the number of shares owned in that Company automatically. Some companies return profit payouts in the form of dividends to their shareholders. This can be as often as quarterly, annually, or by vote of the Board of Directors. Instead of taking the dividend payout in cash, you can choose to use them to automatically purchase more of the Company stock.

When you purchase stock, normally there is an option to reinvest your dividends. Once these dividends are paid to you, the brokerage company will use that money to buy more of that same stock at the current price. Think of it as an automatic purchase of more shares. This helps you to automatically reinvest in that company. Over time, the number of shares can grow significantly based on this simple reinvestment rule. Tip: some brokerage firms allow you to set up dividend reinvestment rules across the board for all your stock purchases. Thus, allowing you to "set it and forget it."

Summary

The "set it and forget it" approach allows you to build your wealth on a schedule and without much interaction. Scheduling purchases through dollar-cost averaging and dividend reimbursements can make investing systematic. The longer you invest, the more likely your wealth can grow.

Establishing Credit for the Future

Tip 12: Understand how credit works

AT SOME POINT IN YOUR life, you will want to lease a car, be on a cell phone plan, rent an apartment, or make a big purchase like buying a house. Most of these situations require the use of credit. Let's discuss how starting now to build your credit, but not necessarily using credit, can help make it easier for you to make those bigger purchases in the future.

What is credit?

Credit is when a vendor is willing to allow you access to an asset (like an apartment, car, etc.) without paying for it in full upfront. Although there are many forms of credit, there are three basic types of credit that will cover most of your credit questions.

Credit cards: Credit cards allow you to borrow money and pay it back later, often with extremely high interest. Credit cards can be an effective way to build your credit history. Some credit cards even allow you to earn rewards, such as cashback or travel points. However, it's important to use credit cards responsibly and pay your bill in full each month to avoid paying exorbitant interest.

Personal credit lines: Personal lines of credit are like credit cards, whereas they also offer a revolving credit limit, which means you can borrow money up to your credit limit and repay it as you need to. Personal lines of credit can be a helpful way to cover unexpected expenses or make large purchases. An example of this is monthly mobile phone contracts.

Installment loans attached to an asset: Installment loans are loans that are repaid over a fixed length of time with equal consistent payments made each month. The vendor holds a "lien" or rights of ownership on the related asset until the loan and computed interest is paid in full. Installment loans can be used for a variety of purposes, such as buying a car or a house.

Working with the credit limit

As you see, credit is borrowing funds with a promise to pay them back. Most credit cards and personal credit lines have a limit on the amount of funds they will allow you to use. This is called the credit limit or credit ceiling. If you hit this credit limit, you will not be able to use the credit card anymore until you pay down your balance. This credit limit is revolving so once you pay down your balance, you can continue to "borrow" on the credit card up to your credit limit. Everyone's credit limit is different and dependent on their credit score.

Understanding the credit score

When you are making a large purchase or long-term rental, the vendor must determine whether you are trustworthy enough to pay them back for the release of that asset. Normally they will "run a credit check" or get your "credit score." A good credit score can help you get a lower interest rate on loans, such as mortgages and car loans. It can also help you qualify for credit cards and other forms of credit.

A credit score is a number computed by the three main credit bureaus on how reliable a person has been in the past with paying off their loans. It is based on a variety of factors, including your timeliness of payments, the amount of debt you hold, and the length of your credit history. The range goes from 0 to 850. The higher the number, the better. Here are some general tips on your credit score.

- Average scores range from 300 to 850. A score of 720 or higher is considered good.
- Your credit score is not the only factor that lenders consider when making lending decisions. They will also look at your income, employment history, and debt-to-income ratio.
- Your ability to keep your open credit in good standing adds to a higher score. On the flip side, late or no payment adversely affects your credit score.
- You can get a free copy of your credit report from each of the three major credit bureaus once a year at https://www.annualcreditreport.com.[5]
- You can dispute any errors in your credit report by contacting the credit bureau that reported the error.

This scenario of building credit seems like a catch-22. You can't qualify for credit without a good credit history. You can't build a good credit history without first qualifying for credit. Not to worry. Let's look at a strategy to do it.

Improving your credit score

Here are some tips to improve your credit score:

1. Make all your payments on time. This is a key factor in determining your credit score.
2. Keep your credit utilization low. Aim to use less than 30% of your available credit.
3. Increase the length of your credit history. The longer you have a good credit history, the better your score will be.
4. Avoid applying for too much credit. Too many inquiries can lower your score.

Summary

At some point in life, most people will need to use credit. This could be as simple as getting a cell phone plan or a credit card. Building a strong credit history and working on improving your credit score are essential steps. Having a higher credit score can help you qualify for better terms on future loans and other forms of credit, like a car loan or home mortgage, when you most need it.

Tip 13: Get a starter credit card

AFTER YOU HAVE ABOUT 6 months of employment history, start applying for your first credit card. Employment can be past summer or part-time jobs. The time employed should be consistent. Since you are just starting on your credit building journey, here are some tips when selecting a first credit card.

Applying for a starter card

First, select a "no annual fee" credit card. To get a higher credit score, you will need to show a steady credit history of over four years. Also, the credit bureaus tend to factor in how long you have kept your oldest credit. The longer you can hold an open credit card and keep it in good standing, the better your overall credit score. Thus, having a no-annual-fee credit card will allow you to keep that credit card for as long as you live without paying any fees.

The second is to select a card that targets college students or young adults. Some examples are Discover card or Chase Freedom. These are just options, and I am not recommending them exclusively over other credit cards. These cards are known as starter cards. They tend to be more understanding with an applicant's earned income. The main reason I suggest these starter cards is that they tend to be easier to get approval. If approved, they tend to have low credit limits ranging from several hundred to a thousand dollars. Because your credit is just starting, the credit card companies want to limit their risk exposure should you default or not pay back what you borrowed.

Another good option for your first credit card is to work with your local bank. If you have been banking at the same bank for over four years, ask the banker at your local branch to assist you with opening a no-annual-fee credit card. Personal bankers have a goal of establishing long-term relationships with their local customers. Often, they have a little more flexibility in approving a credit card for someone they know or feel they can vouch for. This is also a fantastic way to establish a working relationship with a personal banker. That relationship is an advantage to wealth building in the future.

How to use this starter credit card

Many young adults tell me they love using their debit cards for everyday purchases because they are fearful of overextending themselves on credit. That is a valid point. The main pitfall of having credit is spending more. I want to reiterate that the purpose of this credit card is to help establish that minimum of four years of good credit history. Having credit does not mean you need to use it to the full credit ceiling. What the credit bureaus are looking for is a trend of paying back loans in a consistent and timely manner. Do you have a history of paying off all your credit cards on time? Do you tend to use your credit, but not max out the credit ceiling consistently? Do you pay down your balances more? Thus, you are going to build your credit history by not spending more but spending it on things you have already budgeted for and paying it off every month.

Be aware of these unique credit card fees

While using your first credit card, there may be some fees related to using it. Two fees that are important to avoid are:

1. **Foreign transaction fee:** If you use your credit card in a foreign country or purchase in foreign currency, the credit card company may attach a fee associated with the purchase. This charge is to offset the cost of converting the purchase from the foreign currency to your country's currency. It is commonly assessed as an additional percentage of the purchase price. I have seen fees ranging from 1% - 3%.
2. **Cash advance fee**: A credit card is normally used at a vendor. If you choose to withdraw cash from your credit card instead, the credit card company may attach a fee. This charge helps to offset their lost transaction income from the vendor. It is commonly assessed as an additional percentage of the withdrawal with a minimum cost (i.e. 5% with a minimum of $15.00).

One surprising cash advance pitfall involves cash transfer apps. These apps (i.e. Venmo, Zelle, etc.) may allow you to link your credit card. However, using that credit card to send money to a friend may trigger the cash advance fee for the credit card, and possibly an additional one from the app itself. [6]

Knowing about these unique fees can help you plan ahead. If you expect to make purchases abroad, it is ideal to also look for credit cards that have no annual fee but also offer no foreign transaction fees. If your credit card does have a cash advance fee, avoid using that credit card for person-to-person cash transfers in cash transfer apps.

Summary

Getting a starter credit card is a smart way to begin building your credit history. Choosing one with no annual fee credit card makes it easier to keep it long term, which helps to build a longer credit history. If you plan to use it abroad, select one that also has no foreign transaction fees. One notable pitfall is to avoid using these credit cards for cash advances which can have high associated fees. Choosing the right starter card and using it wisely can help lay that solid foundation for a stronger credit profile in the future.

Tip 14: Use credit wisely

THE RISK OF OVERSPENDING with a credit card is real. If you start to carry over your credit card balances, it can easily spiral out of hand. This is due to the financing interest expense you will be assessed to carry over that balance.

The overspending risks

Credit card companies charge exorbitantly high financing interest rates. For example, some current sample annual credit card interest rates are in the 14.99% to 22.99% range. I have seen some as high as 26%. Worse, this finance interest charge is cumulative. Meaning, you are charged this interest rate on top of your item purchased plus any interest charges previously charged. This is hard to visualize how much it can snowball into something unmanageable.

For simplicity, let's look at a $1,000.00 purchase that is not paid off until month 12 or 24.

Annual interest rate:		20%
Purchase amount:	$	1,000.00
Total interest paid:	$	486.91

month	interest	balance
0	$ -	$ 1,000.00
1	$ 16.67	$ 1,016.67
2	$ 16.94	$ 1,033.61
3	$ 17.23	$ 1,050.84
4	$ 17.51	$ 1,068.35
5	$ 17.81	$ 1,086.16
6	$ 18.10	$ 1,104.26
7	$ 18.40	$ 1,122.66
8	$ 18.71	$ 1,141.38
9	$ 19.02	$ 1,160.40
10	$ 19.34	$ 1,179.74
11	$ 19.66	$ 1,199.40
12	$ 19.99	$ 1,219.39
13	$ 20.32	$ 1,239.71
14	$ 20.66	$ 1,260.38
15	$ 21.01	$ 1,281.38
16	$ 21.36	$ 1,302.74
17	$ 21.71	$ 1,324.45
18	$ 22.07	$ 1,346.53
19	$ 22.44	$ 1,368.97
20	$ 22.82	$ 1,391.78
21	$ 23.20	$ 1,414.98
22	$ 23.58	$ 1,438.56
23	$ 23.98	$ 1,462.54
24	$ 24.38	$ 1,486.91

As you can see from the table above, items that are purchased at $1,000.00 end up costing $1,219.39 by month 12 and $1,486.91 by month 24.

Let's see another scenario. When you carry a credit card balance, credit card companies normally require you to pay a low minimum monthly balance. For simplicity, let's look at a $1,000.00 purchase where only the $25.00 minimum balance is paid monthly.

Annual interest rate:	20%
Purchase amount:	$ 1,000.00
Total interest paid:	$ 714.24

month	interest	minimum paid	balance
0	$ -	$ (25.00)	$ 1,025.00
1	$ 17.08	$ (25.00)	$ 1,017.08
2	$ 16.95	$ (25.00)	$ 1,009.03
3	$ 16.82	$ (25.00)	$ 1,000.85
4	$ 16.68	$ (25.00)	$ 992.53
5	$ 16.54	$ (25.00)	$ 984.08
6	$ 16.40	$ (25.00)	$ 975.48
7	$ 16.26	$ (25.00)	$ 966.73
8	$ 16.11	$ (25.00)	$ 957.85
9	$ 15.96	$ (25.00)	$ 948.81
10	$ 15.81	$ (25.00)	$ 939.62
11	$ 15.66	$ (25.00)	$ 930.28
12	$ 15.50	$ (25.00)	$ 920.79
13	$ 15.35	$ (25.00)	$ 911.14
14	$ 15.19	$ (25.00)	$ 901.32
15	$ 15.02	$ (25.00)	$ 891.34
16	$ 14.86	$ (25.00)	$ 881.20
17	$ 14.69	$ (25.00)	$ 870.89
18	$ 14.51	$ (25.00)	$ 860.40
19	$ 14.34	$ (25.00)	$ 849.74
20	$ 14.16	$ (25.00)	$ 838.90
21	$ 13.98	$ (25.00)	$ 827.88
22	$ 13.80	$ (25.00)	$ 816.68
23	$ 13.61	$ (25.00)	$ 805.29
24	$ 13.42	$ (25.00)	$ 793.72
25	$ 13.23	$ (25.00)	$ 781.94
26	$ 13.03	$ (25.00)	$ 769.98
27	$ 12.83	$ (25.00)	$ 757.81
28	$ 12.63	$ (25.00)	$ 745.44
29	$ 12.42	$ (25.00)	$ 732.86
30	$ 12.21	$ (25.00)	$ 720.08
31	$ 12.00	$ (25.00)	$ 707.08
32	$ 11.78	$ (25.00)	$ 693.86
33	$ 11.56	$ (25.00)	$ 680.43
34	$ 11.34	$ (25.00)	$ 666.77
35	$ 11.11	$ (25.00)	$ 652.88
36	$ 10.88	$ (25.00)	$ 638.76
37	$ 10.65	$ (25.00)	$ 624.41
38	$ 10.41	$ (25.00)	$ 609.82
39	$ 10.16	$ (25.00)	$ 594.98
40	$ 9.92	$ (25.00)	$ 579.90
41	$ 9.66	$ (25.00)	$ 564.56
42	$ 9.41	$ (25.00)	$ 548.97
43	$ 9.15	$ (25.00)	$ 533.12
44	$ 8.89	$ (25.00)	$ 517.00
45	$ 8.62	$ (25.00)	$ 500.62
46	$ 8.34	$ (25.00)	$ 483.97
47	$ 8.07	$ (25.00)	$ 467.03
48	$ 7.78	$ (25.00)	$ 449.82
49	$ 7.50	$ (25.00)	$ 432.31
50	$ 7.21	$ (25.00)	$ 414.52
51	$ 6.91	$ (25.00)	$ 396.43
52	$ 6.61	$ (25.00)	$ 378.03
53	$ 6.30	$ (25.00)	$ 359.33
54	$ 5.99	$ (25.00)	$ 340.32
55	$ 5.67	$ (25.00)	$ 320.99
56	$ 5.35	$ (25.00)	$ 301.34
57	$ 5.02	$ (25.00)	$ 281.37
58	$ 4.69	$ (25.00)	$ 261.06
59	$ 4.35	$ (25.00)	$ 240.41
60	$ 4.01	$ (25.00)	$ 219.41
61	$ 3.66	$ (25.00)	$ 198.07
62	$ 3.30	$ (25.00)	$ 176.37
63	$ 2.94	$ (25.00)	$ 154.31
64	$ 2.57	$ (25.00)	$ 131.88
65	$ 2.20	$ (25.00)	$ 109.08
66	$ 1.82	$ (25.00)	$ 85.90
67	$ 1.43	$ (25.00)	$ 62.33
68	$ 1.04	$ (25.00)	$ 38.37
69	$ 0.64	$ (25.00)	$ 14.01
70	$ 0.23	$ (14.24)	$ -

As you can see from the table above, it would take 70 months (around 5.8 years) of the minimum payment to pay off this purchase. Items that were initially purchased at $1,000.00 end up costing $1,714.24 ($1000.00 purchase price + $714.24 interest).

I just want to reiterate the purpose of this credit card is to build your foundation for your future credit needs. Rising credit balances can have a negative effect on your credit score. Save yourself the stress of rebuilding your credit by making it a habit of staying within your budget and paying off your monthly credit card amount. The goal is not to "use" the credit but to "build" credit for bigger wealth assets later.

Using it only for "needs"

The best way to use this credit card is to use it for your "needs" bucket expenses. It could replace your debit card for paying for your general needs like groceries, gas, medical copays, etc. as mentioned in Chapter 1. Starting by using it only for your "needs" will help you avoid some pitfalls of overspending on credit. These are expenses that you have normally budgeted for.

When you start the transition from a debit card to a credit card, there will be a slight learning curve. With a debit card, some users have already been conditioned to watch their cash balance. With a credit card, there is no cash balance to watch, but there is a "spend" balance. When converting to using a credit card, you will need to know your needs budget for the month and try to stay within that range for the statement range. Most credit cards issue their statements monthly. Like your debit card, keep all your receipts from your charges in paper or digital form for your monthly reconciliation.

Pro tip: Watching that spend balance is easy by downloading and using your respective credit card app.

Summary

Credit is a tool that can be used to your advantage. It also has temptations to overspend. At the beginning stages of building credit, using credit responsibly and paying it off on time can lay the foundations for a stronger credit history. One effective strategy is establishing a starter credit card to replace your debit card to cover your "needs" bucket. The key to managing credit is to stay within your designated budget and pay off the credit in full monthly, just like you would have if you used a debit card.

Tip 15: Set up credit card autopay

THE NEXT STEP IS TO automate the monthly payoff of the full credit card balance from your checking account. Automating this step helps to ensure that you are paying your credit card on time. The credit card bureaus will review your timely payment to determine your ability to keep your open credit in good standing.

Yes, I did say that the monthly payoff would be the full statement balance. Since you are using this credit card for "needs" only and are staying within your budget, it is merely a replacement for your "needs" debit card payments. You should be able to pay it off fully every month. The benefits of paying the statement balance in full monthly are:

- Renewal of credit limit monthly: Since starter credit cards normally begin with low credit lines (several hundred to a thousand dollars), paying off the monthly statements will allow revolving use of the full credit line again once payment is made.
- Reducing the risk of overspending pitfall: Monthly payoff helps you to monitor your spending and stay within budget.

- Lengthen the period of timely payments: Having renewal of the credit line monthly allows for a systematic on-time payment towards your steady four-year history.
- Avoidance of paying interest: credit card companies will give you a grace period (the average is a month) to pay off the balance before charging the dreaded finance interest. If you carry over any balance over to the next statement, the credit card companies will charge you financing interest to use their funds. As we discussed in Tip #14, avoiding high interest rates is important in using credit wisely.

How to set up autopay

The easiest way to set up autopay is through the respective credit card website or app. Normally there is an option to set up autopay. Here you can designate:

- Bank account to draw from
- Amount: If your intention is to pay off the credit statement monthly, select the statement balance as the amount.
- Date of payment: I suggest selecting at least 2 to 5 days prior to the statement due date. This should provide you time to resolve any banking issues before the due date.

Summary

The "set it and forget it" theory works here as well. Setting up the autopay on this credit card will draw out your monthly "needs" expenses, just like your debit card or autopay used to. Putting this task on autopilot will help to build toward your four-year history of timely payments.

Tip 16: Protect your credit score

NOW THAT YOU HAVE TAKEN the steps to build up this credit, it is a good idea to track your progression annually. This is easily done through the current three main credit bureaus: Equifax, TransUnion, and Experian.

Monitoring your credit

Under the Fair and Accurate Credit Transaction Act, consumers in the USA are allowed to review their credit file for free at least once a year or when they have been a victim of fraud[7]. You can obtain your free credit report on the website www.annualcreditreport.com. You should review all three reports annually or at the very least alternate between them every other year. All bureaus are independent of each other, and some may have different information.

As you read through the reports, take notes of anything that you do not recognize or look suspicious. Examples of common errors to note are below:

- Misspelled names (including middle initials).
  Because there are multiple people with similar names,

minor differences in spelling are important.
- Unrecognized addresses on file
- Unrecognized open loans
- Unrecognized credit cards

Catching and fixing these errors early can help deter bad actors from creeping false information onto your credit and stealing your identity. If you find any errors, contact that specific bureau to have them corrected.

Lock / Freeze your file

All three credit bureaus have online tools that allow you to lock / freeze and unlock / unfreeze your credit file from credit checks. Locking your file is easier and in real time but some bureaus may may charge a fee. Freezing your file is more cumbersome and can take a longer time to activate, but it is free. Both methods restrict access to your credit file so you can choose either method.

If your file is locked / frozen, that means no one should be able to request credit access on you without your approval. Restricting credit access hinders thieves from trying to open loans or credit cards in your name. Should you ever want to apply for credit, be sure to unlock / unfreeze your credit file before your application and lock / freeze it after the credit check. Since the three credit bureaus operate independently and if you are not aware of which bureau the vendor is using, you will need to unlock / unfreeze all three simultaneously. Normally, a credit check can be run instantly, within the day of your application, or a couple of days. This depends on the vendor you are opening credit with.

If you are using credit locks, a good idea is to speak with the vendor on the phone while you unlock and lock your credit to limit your risk of unlocked credit. Just be sure to lock your file with all the open credit bureaus after the credit check is completed.

Placing a credit breach notification

If a vendor notifies you that your personal data, also known as PII (Personal Identifying Information), has been compromised, you are eligible to place a fraud notification on your credit file with the three credit bureaus[8]. If anyone (including you) tries to open a credit card or loan in your name, that credit request will be flagged and placed on hold. The credit bureau will not release the credit report to the vendor until that bureau contacts you (normally via mail) and confirms that you applied for the credit. Note again that because all three bureaus are independent, notification must be made at all three bureaus. The only hassle with this is you cannot open a credit card or apply for credit instantly. On average, it will take a couple of weeks to get that credit application verified.

Signing up for credit monitoring

Why can't I just pay someone to do this for me? You can. There are companies that specialize in credit monitoring. All three credit bureaus offer their own version of credit monitoring. They will send you notifications on credit score changes, new credit applications, who requested a credit check report, and if there were changes to personal information on your credit report. The monitoring usually comes with assistance to clear up credit report errors and with canceling credit cards should they be stolen. It is entirely up to you if the cost is worth it for you. Personally, it is nice to have but not necessarily a need if you follow the steps above. I have found that many banks, credit cards, and associations may offer some type of low-cost credit monitoring for their customers. Be aware that many companies are offering this service, but not all are reputable. Because you will need to reveal PII to them, I recommend only going with one of the three bureaus or your bank for this.

Summary

Building your credit is investing in your future. It will take about four years to get your credit established. Monitor your credit history annually for suspicious or erroneous entries. Protect unauthorized access to you history by freezing your credit with all three credit bureaus when you are not applying for credit. Once you can maintain a high credit score, it will be so much easier to build your wealth for those larger purchases like a home.

Protecting with Insurance

Tip 17: Understand insurance options

LIFE HAPPENS. BECAUSE unforeseen medical expenses can strain financial assets, the focus of insurance is on asset protection. Insurance transfers the risk of unexpected expense to the insurance company in exchange for your monthly contribution known as a premium. Multiple types of insurance are available. This chapter covers the common insurance types offered by an employer.

When you are in your twenties or start working full-time, the furthest thing from your mind is insurance. Within the first thirty days of full-time employment, your employer may present you with a plethora of insurance options. On top of these options, some may be subsidized by your employer, and some paid by you. My goal here is to provide you with the basic information and details to help you decide which is right for you.

Below is a table of some of the most common insurance options that employers may present to you and who normally pays for the insurance. Note: this table is an example and not all-inclusive. Check with your employer about your specific offerings and qualifications as they may differ depending on State or employer policy.

Insurance	Description	Who normally pays?
Medical (may includes prescription drugs)	Medical supplement coverage that normally includes: physician, pharmacy, laboratory, hospital, urgent care, sometimes chiropractor and acupuncture.	Depends on the Company and State Policy: Either Employer 100%, or part employer and employee.
Dental	Dental supplemental coverage that normally includes: bi-annual checkups, a portion of dental repairs for crowns, and cavities, a portion of dental surgery like root canals, and possible orthodontics.	Depends on the Company and State Policy: Either Employer 100%, part employer and employee, or 100% employee.
Vision	Vision supplemental coverage for eyeglasses and contacts.	Depends on the Company and State Policy: Either Employer 100%, part employer and employee, or 100% employee.
Life insurance	Determined payout to beneficiaries upon confirmed death of covered individual	Depends on the Company policy. Normally, the Company will purchase a small insurance policy for the employee but offer a supplemental higher policy payout as an option for purchase by the employee.
Flexible Spending Account	Option to pay for qualified medical out of pocket expenses not covered by insurance (ie. co-pay, deductibles) with pre-tax money.	Employee
Healthcare Savings Account	Option to pay for qualified medical out-of-pocket expenses not covered by insurance (ie. co-pay, deductibles) with pre-tax money. This is only offered if the employee selects a high-deductible medical health plan.	Depends on the Company and State Policy: Either part employer and employee, or 100% employee.
Non work related Accident and disability	Monthly payment benefits should covered individual suffer a non-work accident or disability and can no longer perform their current work at the same level.	Employee
Temporary Disability	Monthly payment benefits to cover temporary leave from work for a medical issue. This is most common used for family leave after birth.	Employer
Other specific situation insurance (I.e. cancer, pet,etc.)	Monthly payment benefits dependent upon specific event happening (i.e. cancer, pet illness, etc.)	Employee

When do I sign up?

There are three common sign-up periods:

1. The first is after you are hired and meet the employer's designated number of working hours. Most commonly it is four weeks after employment if you work a minimum of twenty hours a week. This depends on your state law and employer. You should be informed of this insurance option when you are onboarded at your company.
2. The second sign-up period is called "open enrollment." This is the annual companywide enrollment period that happens once a year. It is also the time when you can make changes to your existing insurance selections.
3. The third sign-up period is during significant life changes. This includes marriage, divorce, having a child, or the death of an existing plan participant, etc.

Otherwise, once you select your option, you are tied to that selection until the next open enrollment period or when you leave employment (voluntarily or involuntarily).

How do I sign up?

Your employer will notify you when you have met the employer's designated working hours or during open enrollment. If you had a significant life change, then you would notify your employer's human resource department to address the addition or deletion of dependents. In all cases, you will typically have 30 days from notification to sign up.

Who can I sign up?

The qualifying employee is always eligible to sign up for insurance offered. Qualification is usually determined by the State and then employer rules. More than likely, the employer will subsidize part of the employee's monthly medical insurance payment. It is also common for the employer to offer coverage for your immediate family (spouse, dependent, or children) at a cost. Sometimes, as a retention incentive, the employer will also subsidize part of the dependent or family medical. That scenario is rare but a nice perk when you have a family. It is best to check with your employer as to what coverage options they offer.

What should I sign up for?

Yes, there are so many options. Aside from medical and dental, be mindful and select only what you guess you will need as most other insurance is paid for by the employee. Your selection can take a considerable chunk of your net paycheck.

1. **Medical is a must.** I hope that you are among the percentage of individuals who do not need to deal with medical issues or their looming bills. Most employers will offer the opportunity to purchase medical insurance for you as an employee and

sometimes your family. The thought process behind medical insurance is this. For a monthly premium paid to the insurer, the covered individual(s) out-of-pocket expenses for covered medical procedures and prescriptions are limited to a predetermined out-of-pocket amount. Select whichever plan best fits your needs and budget.

2. **Dental is a must.** Dental insurance is recommended coverage because dental care is expensive. Most plans will cover your basic preventative semiannual checkup and cleaning. Any additional treatments (think cavity filling, crowns, root canals, wisdom teeth extraction, etc.) will normally only be covered as a percentage. The rest would be out of pocket. Selecting a predefined network of dentists (a.k.a. HMO) will save you money on insurance but will limit the choice of dentists you can see. If you do not expect large dental work in the future and do not have a favorite dentist (or your current dentist participates in the plan), this HMO plan may be fine for you. I have found that if you expect to do large dental work that involves dental surgery (i.e., root canals and wisdom teeth), a dental plan with a PPO will give you more options for selecting a provider. Select whichever plan best fits your needs and budget.

3. **The rest are optional.** Adding the remainder of the

employer insurance options offered depend upon your situation. The remainder of the insurance will usually be paid for by the employee only. Granted that you may be able to use pre-tax money to cover the monthly premium, the cumulative effect of paying for these specific insurance options will take a chunk out of your net paycheck. Specific insurance like long-term disability, accident, or pet insurance is useful if any of those situations are a main concern to you. You normally do not need all the other insurance unless your specific situation calls for it (i.e., extra life insurance to pay off a mortgage in the event of your demise, pet insurance, accident insurance if you participate in extreme sports).

Summary

Insurance by its very definition is a protection plan. You want just enough to help you sleep at night, but not too much to drain your wallet. Something to set and revisit usually once a year. Having it set should give you peace of mind that you are covered for a major issue should something unexpected occur.

Tip 18: Save on healthcare

IF YOU ANTICIPATE HAVING a set amount of medical expenses or anticipate not having any excessive medical expenses, there are some wealth-saving options allowed in the United States under the Flexible Spending Account (FSA) and Healthcare Savings Account (HSA).

Flexible Spending Account (FSA)

A flexible spending account (FSA) is a pre-tax account that allows you to set aside money from your paycheck to pay for qualified medical expenses. You can use the money in your FSA to pay for qualified expenses like doctor's visits, prescription drugs, and medical supplies. FSAs are only offered through an employer.

The money you contribute to your FSA is deducted from your paycheck before taxes are taken out, which means you save money on your taxes. If you are in the average 30% tax bracket for Federal plus State combined, you are essentially getting 30% off your copay or out-of-pocket expenses for your doctor visits, eyeglasses, medicine, dental work, and the like. If you have a lot of medical expenses expected for the calendar year, FSAs are a terrific way to save money on your healthcare costs.

Normally, FSA accounts must be used within the plan year, or the funds will expire (a.k.a. use it or lose it). If selected by your employer, there is the option that a portion of unused FSA funds may be rolled over to the next year for up to 2.5 months after the plan year-end. The amount that can be rolled over and for what length of time is determined by the Internal Revenue Service and your employer elections to allow the rollover.[9] Please check with your employer if they allow this rollover.

Healthcare Savings Account (HSA)

A healthcare savings plan is also a tax-deferred account. It can be funded by the employer, employee, or both. To open this account, you must select a high-deductible health plan (HDHP), and you may not have any other health coverage for that plan year. HDHPs normally have lower monthly premiums than traditional health plans, but you may pay more out-of-pocket deductibles for your medical expenses before your insurance kicks in. The definition of what qualifies as an HDHP can change according to the Internal Revenue Service guidelines.[10] Because of the restrictions, it is best to confirm with your health plan provider if your plan is considered HDHP eligible and if you qualify for an HSA.

Although HSAs are limited by the type of health plan you can select, they do have some additional benefits:

- The funds can remain in your tax-deferred account until used for qualified medical expenses. Therefore, the funds do not expire.
- You can invest the funds in a savings account or brokerage account. Any growth in the funds can also be used to pay for qualified medical expenses tax-free. Note: these funds invested are still subject to the risks of growth and loss of the underlying investment (i.e., equities, bonds, etc.).
- You can still utilize the funds for qualified medical expenses in subsequent years even though you are no longer eligibly enrolled in an HDHP.

When to add an FSA or HSA

Below are general tips on when to add each option:

FSA: Consider adding a Flexible Spending Account if you expect to have a planned medical expense with higher copayment amounts (i.e. wisdom teeth, knee surgery, etc.) or fixed annual medical expenses (like contacts and prescription medicine). FSAs are ideal if you want the flexibility to choose from a variety of your employer's health plans. Because the funds expire annually, I recommend contributing only the amount you are sure to spend or less than 85% of your anticipated qualifying expenses. This will help with balancing maximizing your tax benefit, while not overcontributing.

HSA: Consider adding a Health Savings Account if you are healthy, rarely use costly healthcare (i.e. emergency room visits, imaging, hospital stays, high prescription drugs, etc.), and want to save tax-deferred funds to use towards future qualified medical expenses. The real drawback to an HSA is the limitation on the type of High-Deductible Health Plan that you can select to qualify for an HSA. Because determining your healthcare usage is difficult to foresee, ensure that you have enough emergency funds to cover your deductibles and copays before selecting a High-Deductible Health Plan for your medical coverage. Because of the limitation on the health plan selection, I am not a strong proponent of the HSA.

Summary

The primary goal of insurance is to provide you with a financial safety net. Start by selecting the insurance plan that works best for your needs and budget. Then, if you anticipate having set qualified medical expenses or an upcoming large expenditure, consider planning for these known medical expenses through a Flexible Spending Account (FSA). It is a straightforward way of getting a tax-free "discount" on expenses in your "needs" bucket. Insurance in conjunction with an FSA can provide peace of mind protection with some wealth preservation.

Conclusion

MY HOPE IS THAT THIS book gives insight into how to work smarter, not harder. Use the combined power of automation and time as tools to gain control over the management of your money. I find that control brings calm to my financial decision making. This allows me to free up my brain power to invest more energy into what I am passionate about. I hope the same goes for you.

Every small step forward can lead to substantial progress. You don't have to do everything at once—implementing just a few tips from this book can help lay a foundation across the four pillars of personal finance: managing your money wisely, building wealth, strengthening your credit, and protecting it all through insurance. I have seen firsthand how consistent, intentional action can mold someone's financial future. I hope you experience these same rewards. Thank you for letting me be a part of your journey towards financial independence.

Let's stay in touch

DID THIS BOOK HELP you in some way? If so, I'd love to hear about it. Connect with me at www.apairagroup.com[1] or on Instagram or Facebook @apairagroup for future money management tips.

Honest reviews help other readers discover the right book for their needs. If you found this book helpful, consider sharing your thoughts by leaving a review where you purchased it. Your feedback can inspire smarter money decisions and support others on their journey to financial independence. Thank you for your time and your commitment to financial growth.

---

1. http://www.apairagroup.com

Bibliography

§ 1005.6 Liability of consumer for unauthorized transfers. (2023). Retrieved from Consumer Financial Protection Bureau: https://www.consumerfinance.gov/rules-policy/regulations/1005/6/

Fair and Accurate Credit Transactions Act of 2003. (2023). Retrieved from Federal Trade Commission: https://www.ftc.gov/legal-library/browse/statutes/fair-accurate-credit-transactions-act-2003

Federal Deposit Insurance Corporation. (2024, 04 01). *Deposit Insurance.* Retrieved from Deposit Insurance FAQs: https://www.fdic.gov/resources/deposit-insurance/faq

Publication 590-B (2023), Distributions from Individual Retirement Arrangements (IRAs). (2024). Retrieved from IRS: https://www.irs.gov/publications/p590b

Publication 969 (2023), Health Savings Accounts and Other Tax-Favored Health Plans. (2024). Retrieved from IRS: https://www.irs.gov/publications/p969

Traditional and Roth IRAs. (2023). Retrieved from IRS: https://www.irs.gov/retirement-plans/traditional-and-roth-iras

[1] *Electronic Fund Transfer Act 15 USC 1693 et seq. and Regulation E 12 CFR Part 1005 (2023) https://www.consumerfinance.gov/rules-policy/regulations/1005/6/*

[2] *Roth IRAs, 26 U.S. Code § 408A (2024). https://www.irs.gov/publications/p590b#en_US_2023_publink100089543*

[3] *Internal Revenue Service, Publication 915 (2024), Social Security and Equivalent Railroad Retirement Benefits. https://www.irs.gov/publications/p915#en_US_2024_publink100041019*

[4] *Federal Deposit Insurance Corporation. (2024, August 13). Welcome to the FDIC's Electronic Deposit Insurance Estimator (EDIE). https://edie.fdic.gov/index.html*

[5] *Fair and Accurate Credit Transactions Act of 2003, 15 U.S.C. §§ 1681-1681x (2023). https://www.ftc.gov/legal-library/browse/statutes/fair-accurate-credit-transactions-act-2003*

[6] *PayPal, Inc. (2021). Fees with your Venmo Account. https://venmo.com/resources/our-fees/*

[7] *Fair and Accurate Credit Transactions Act of 2003, 15 U.S.C. §§ 1681-1681x (2023). https://www.ftc.gov/legal-library/browse/statutes/fair-accurate-credit-transactions-act-2003*

[8] *Fair and Accurate Credit Transactions Act of 2003, 15 U.S.C. §§ 1681-1681x (2023). https://www.ftc.gov/legal-library/browse/statutes/fair-accurate-credit-transactions-act-2003*

[9] Internal Revenue Code, § 106(c)(2) (2024). https://www.irs.gov/publications/p969#en_US_2023_publink1000204190

[10] Internal Revenue Code, § 223 (2024) ttps://www.irs.gov/publications/p969#en_US_2023_publink1000204025

www.ingramcontent.com/pod-product-compliance
Lightning Source LLC
Chambersburg PA
CBHW062232150726
47991CB00006B/2549